Lion's Mane

To parents Your child will practice cutting short lines with one or two strokes. It is okay if your child goes off the cutting line or cuts unevenly. Please assist your child and keep an eye on him or her to avoid any injuries.

W9-BNO-213

‹ example ›

■ Cut along ▬▬. Start from ⇒.

Sky-High

To parents   Your child will practice repeatly opening and closing scissors to cut longer lines. It is okay for your child to stop after one stroke and start over again. When your child has successfully cut each part out, offer lots of praise.

< example >

■ Cut along ▬▬▬▬. Start from ➡.

Connect the Train Cars

≪ example ≫

To parents   When your child has completed the cutting, encourage him or her to arrange the parts to make a long train.

■ Cut along ▬▬▬▬. Start from ➡.

4 Santa Claus

To parents The lines on this page are diagonal. Don't be concerned if your child's cutting is uneven. When he or she is finished, you and your child can play with the Santa Claus mask and talk about your favorite winter holidays.

◄ example ►

■ Cut along ▭. Start from ➡.

5 Giraffe Family

To parents The lines on this page are longer than earlier exercises. If your child is having difficulty holding the paper steady while cutting, you can place the paper on a table.

< example >

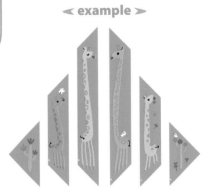

■ Cut along ▬▬▬▬ . Start from ➡ .

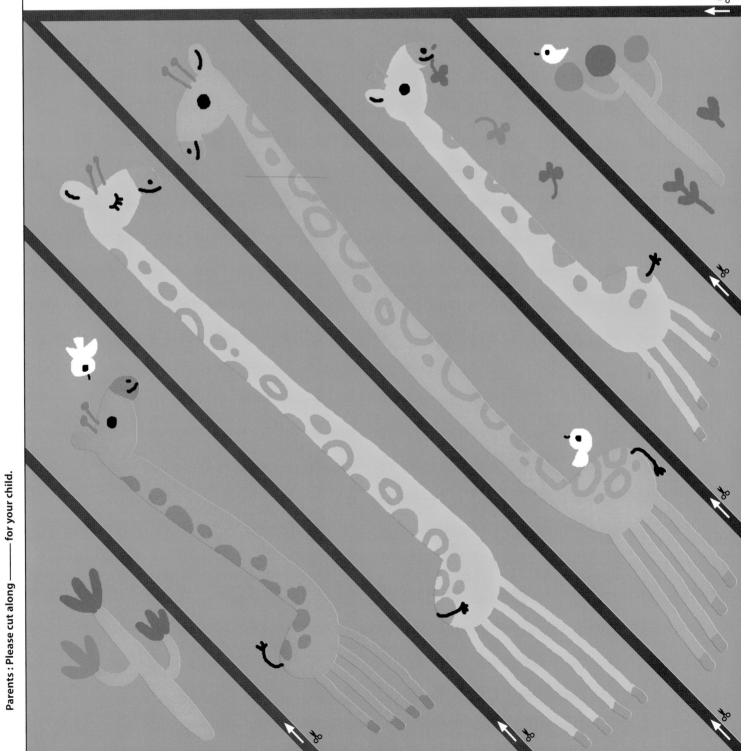

Brush Your Teeth

To parents   Your child will practice cutting out the diamond-shaped mirror. When he or she is finished, say "What is in the mirror?"

■ Cut along ▅▅▅▅. Start from ➡.

Over the Rainbow

To parents In this exercise, your child will practice cutting curving lines. It is okay if your child goes off the line or cuts in straight lines at first. Help your child open and close the scissors with short strokes in order to cut the curves neatly.

≺ example ≻

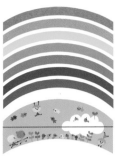

■ Cut along ▬▬▬. Start from ➡.

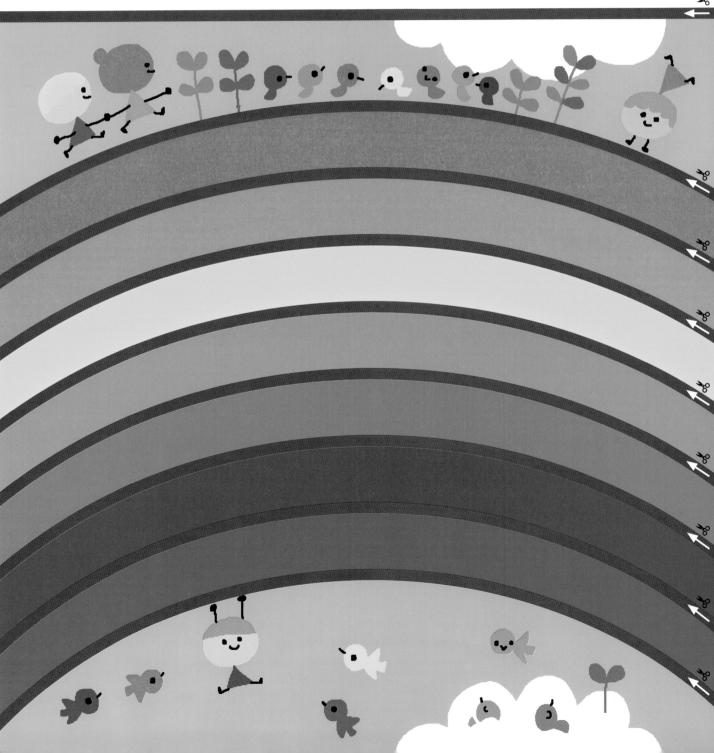

Parents : Please cut along ——— for your child.

8 Climb a Mountain

To parents   On this page, the curving lines are more difficult. Encourage your child to cut curves slowly and steadily. When he or she has successfully cut the paper, offer lots of praise.

< example >

■ Cut along ▬▬▬▬ . Start from ➡ .

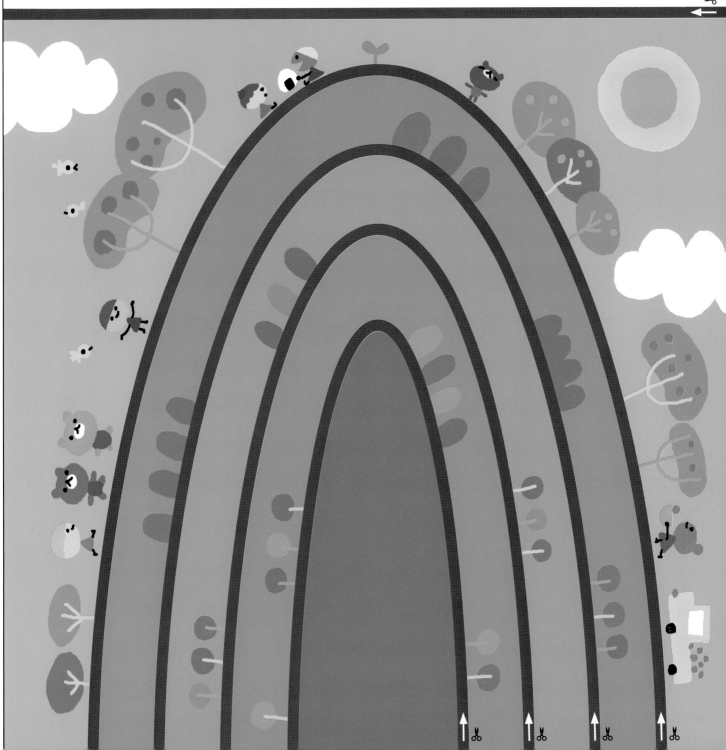

Parents : Please cut along ———— for your child.

9 Slice the Cake

To parents First your child will cut out the whole cake and then, slice it. When he or she is finished, you can pretend you are eating the cake.

< example >

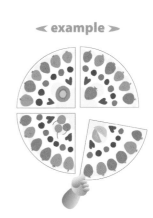

■ Cut along ▬▬▬▬. Start from ▬▶.

Lobsters

≪ example ≫

To parents Cutting in a zigzag is a difficult skill to master. When your child has successfully cut the paper, offer lots of praise. You can also have fun by fighting the lobsters.

■ Cut along ▭▭▭ . Start from ⇒ .

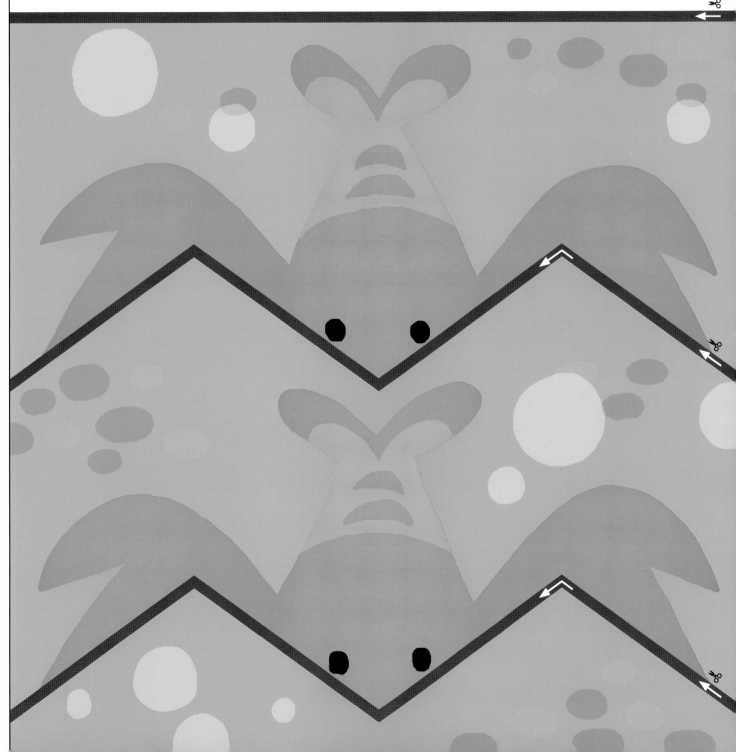

Gorilla

≺ example ≻

To parents When your child has completed the exercise, you can show the gorilla eating the banana with his sharp teeth.

■ Cut along ▬▬▬. Start from ➡.

12 Beautiful Dress

To parents In this exercise, your child will practice cutting wavy curves. It is okay for him or her to cut sharper angles at first. Remind your child to change direction a bit with each short stroke.

≺ example ≻

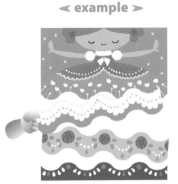

■ Cut along ▬▬▬▬. Start from ➡.

Whale Watching

To parents Help your child open and close the scissors with short strokes in order to cut curves neatly.
Through repeated practice, he or she will acquire stronger scissor control.

≺ example ≻

■ Cut along ▬▬▬▬. Start from ➡.

Parents : Please cut along ——— for your child.

14 Snake

To parents After your child has cut along the designated lines, hold the end up and let the cut portion fall down in a spiral. You can say something like, "Watch out for the snake!"

≪ example ≫

■ Cut along ▬▬▬▬. Start from ➡.

Let's Go Home

To parents It is important for your child to learn how to hold the paper with one hand while he or she cuts with the other hand. Help your child continue adjusting the paper in the right direction so that he or she is always holding the scissors straight.

Cut along ▬▬▬. Start from ➡.

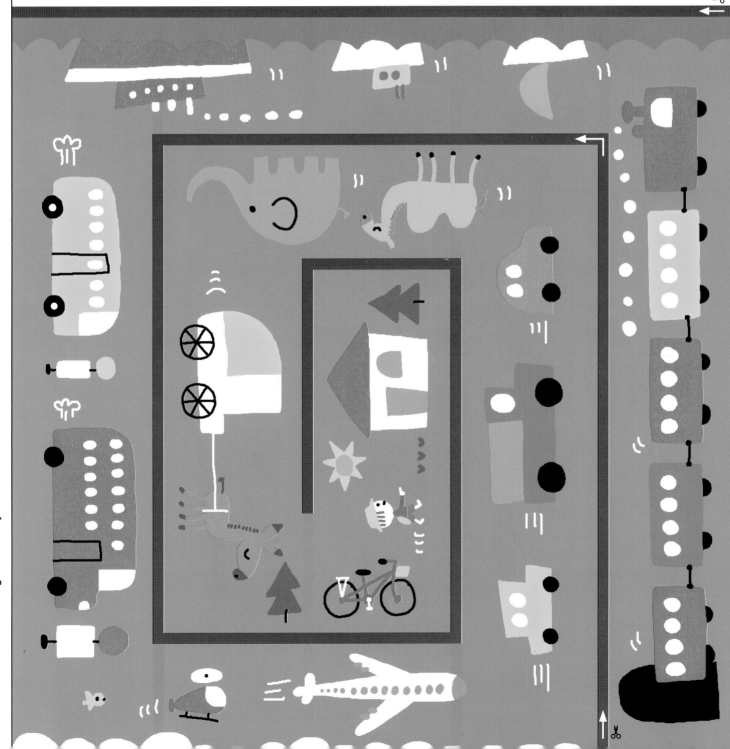

Catching a Fly

To parents In this exercise, your child must hold the paper and turn it while cutting. Make sure he or she is holding the scissors at the proper angle. After the exercise is done, your child can play with the lizard's swirling tongue.

≺ example ≻

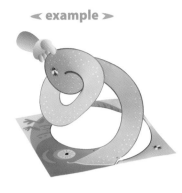

■ Cut along ▬▬▬. Start from ➡.

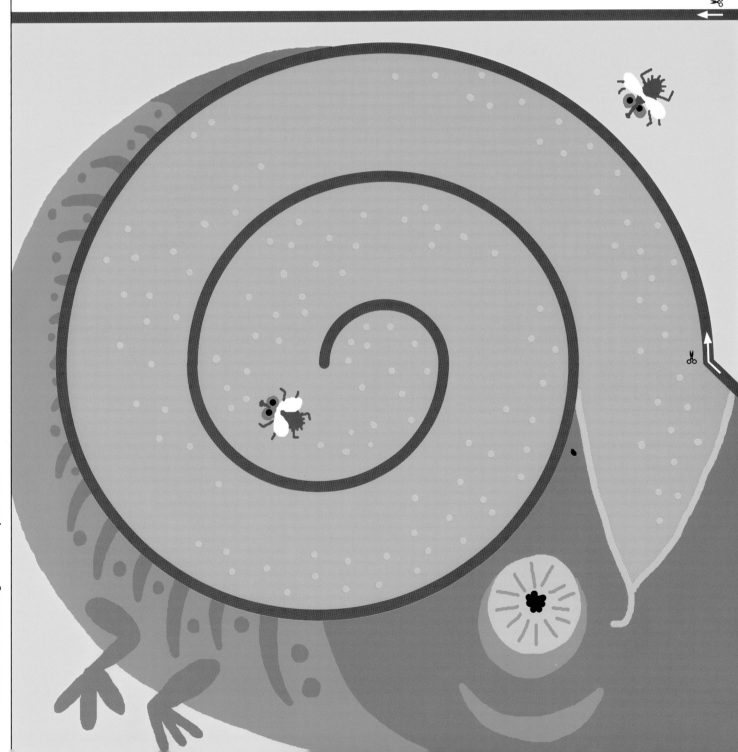

Swirling Noodles

To parents This cutting line is longer than previous exercises. Your child will practice holding and turning the paper with one hand while cutting with the other hand. When your child is finished, offer lots of praise and encourage him or her to play with the swirling noodles.

■ Cut along ▬▬▬. Start from ➡.

18 Breakfast Time

To parents From this page on, your child will cut out some parts. There is no starting line from the edge of the paper. If your child doesn't know where to begin cutting, tell him or her it is okay to start cutting from anywhere.

■ Cut along ▬▬▬▬ .

Lunch For Two

≺ example ≻

To parents   When your child has successfully finished, offer lots of praise. You can also use the pieces to pretend to have lunch with your child.

■ Cut along ▅▅▅▅.

20 Elephant and Orangutan

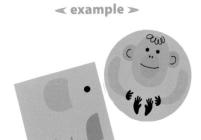

To parents When your child cuts these round shapes, he or she will practice steadily turning the paper while cutting in order to make an evenly curved line. When your child has finished, you can play with the animals and ask, "What sounds do these animals make?"

■ Cut along ▬▬▬ .

Parents : Please cut along ——— for your child.

Track Meet

To parents Don't be concerned if your child goes off the cutting line or cuts unevenly. When he or she is finished, offer lots of praise.

■ Cut along ▬▬▬▬ .

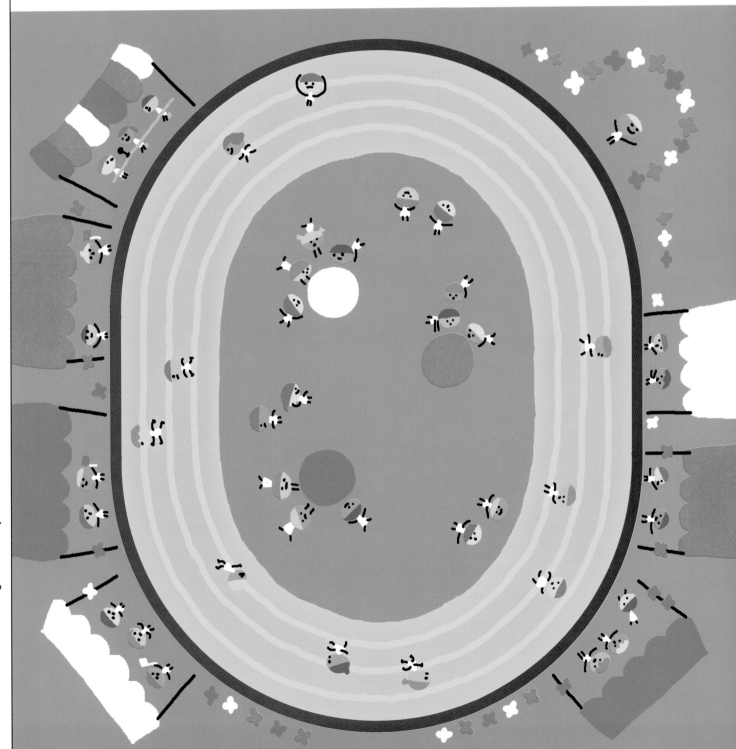

Parents : Please cut along ——— for your child.

Thanksgiving

To parents From this page on, your child will cut out familiar objects. This illustration has an intricate shape. If your child does not cut the turkey perfectly, don't be concerned. When your child is finished, offer a lot of praise.

≪ example ≫

■ Cut along ▬▬▬▬▬ .

23 Halloween

< example >

To parents Please make sure your child is holding the scissors at the proper angle to the paper. Encourage your child to cut the pumpkin slowly and steadily.

■ Cut along ▬▬▬ .

Camping

To parents In this exercise, your child will cut out some parts. If your child doesn't know where to begin cutting, tell him or her it is okay to start from anywhere. When your child is finished, offer him or her a lot of praise and play with the tent's folding flap door.

≪ example ≫

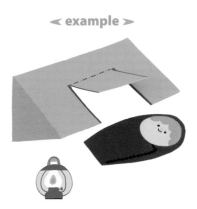

■ Cut along ▬▬▬ and fold along ▬ ·—· .

Christmas Tree

< example >

To parents If your child is cutting into the picture, help him or her adjust the scissor's direction. Even if he or she cuts too far, you can always mend the paper with tape. When the Christmas tree is cut out, display it in your home.

■ Cut along ▬▬▬▬ .

Circus

‹ example ›

To parents   From this page on, each exercise is two pages. Your child will cut out all the parts on the first page, and then he or she can display them in the scene on the second page.

■ Cut along ▰▰▰ and fold along – – – .
Then, stand the parts on the circus stage on the next page.

27 Circus

To parents On this page, your child can place the pieces wherever he or she likes. An example is offered but please allow your child to play freely.

■ Cut along ▬▬▬▬ and fold along —·—·—.

28 Playground

To parents In this exercise, your child will cut out the parts for the playground scene. These illustrations have very intricate shapes. If your child does not cut the shapes perfectly, don't be concerned. You can help him or her cut and fold. When your child is finished, offer a lot of praise.

< example >

■ Cut along ▬▬▬ and fold along – – – .
Then, stand the parts on the playground on the next page.

≪ example ≫

To parents On this page, your child will cut out the setting and place the pieces on the playground. There are many ways to place the pieces. Encourage your child to have fun by placing the parts in different arrangements.

■ Cut along ▬▬▬ and fold along ▬ · ▬ · ▬ .

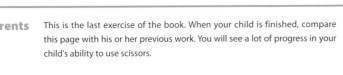

To parents This is the last exercise of the book. When your child is finished, compare this page with his or her previous work. You will see a lot of progress in your child's ability to use scissors.

■ Cut along ▬▬▬ and fold along ‒ ‒ ‒ .
Then, stand the parts on the roundabout on the next page.

31 In Town

To parents Please encourage your child to place the parts wherever he or she likes. When the exercise is finished, remember to praise your child for his or her hard work.

≺ example ≻

■ Cut along ▬▬▬▬.

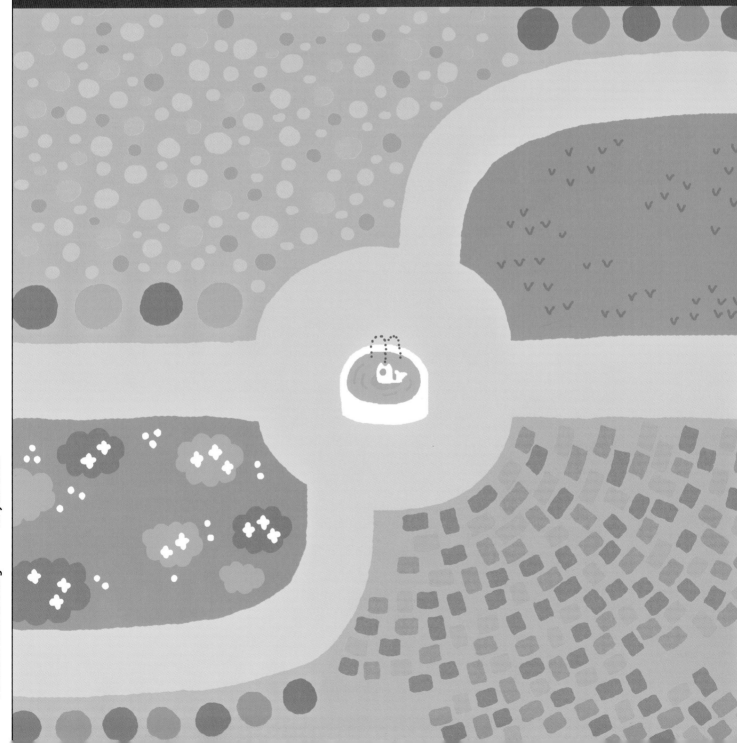

KUM◯N

Certificate of Achievement

is hereby congratulated on completing

Are You Ready for Kindergarten? Scissor Skills

Presented on _____, 20____

_____
Parent or Guardian